Secrets of a Wedding DJ

Theories on song selections and playlists

DJ RICHY ROY

PRESTIGE BOOK PUBLISHING

Library and Archives Canada Cataloguing in Publication

Roy, Richy, author
    Secrets of a wedding DJ : theories in song selections and playlists /
author,
DJ Richy Roy.

ISBN 978-0-9959024-2-8 (hardcover).—ISBN 978-0-9959024-0-4 (softcover)

    1. Disc jockeys--Handbooks, manuals, etc. 2. Disc jockeys--Vocational
guidance. I. Title.

ML3795.R888 2017   781.5'87   C2017-901253-3

THIS IS A GOURAMI BOOK
BY PRESTIGE BOOK PUBLISHING

ISBN: 978-0-9959024-0-4
Printed by CreateSpace
Published February 25, 2017
First Edition

Table of Contents

Introduction   viii

All Wedding DJs Are Not Equal   1

Expectations and the Top 100 Songs   6

The Reception Dance is a Play   8

Building Your Set List(s)   11

    Mini Set Lists by Genre   13

    Mini Set Lists by Mood   19

    Mini Set Lists by Decades   21

    Mini Set Lists by Events   24

    Mini Set Lists by Top 40   27

    DJ Performance Set List   28

Where to Find Songs   29

50,000 Song Library   35

Putting it All Together   37

5pm – Cocktail hour   37

6pm – Grand Entrance   38

6:15pm – Dinner Music   38

7:30pm – First dance (special dances)   38

7:45pm – Open Dancing   39

11:00pm – Midnight Lunch Set   52

1:30am – Last Call Set   53

1:55pm Last Song   56

2:00pm Clean Up   56

Chicken or the Egg?   58

Handling Requests   61

Line Dances and Special Dances   67

Memorable Moments   70

Conclusion   74

Appendix   77

    Top 100 Songs   77

    Line Dances & Special Dance Songs   81

    Last Songs   84

    Grand Entrances   87

Introduction

My name is DJ Richy Roy. I've learnt a lot about DJing weddings (from experience alone) and I'm about to share my secrets that I've learnt, with you. This book will not cover equipment setups, lighting techniques, marketing, promoting, and mixing skills. Those topics are already covered in many other books and I may write my own take on them in the future. This book is all about playing the best set list of music at each and every wedding you perform for. I think this is the single biggest topic that gets left out of most DJ books or courses on the market, yet it is the most important thing that separates the rookies from the experts. I will talk about theories common to all DJs and some new observations I've made on my own from DJing over one hundred weddings. After reading this book, you will be armed with the knowledge of how to put together the best song list, in the best order, and nail that reception each and every time. There is a lot of information put into this small book. Read through it carefully and use these secrets that have taken me many years to learn. Knowledge is useless if one does not actually use it.

All Wedding DJs Are Not Equal

BEFORE we get to the secrets of song selections, I want to talk about the difference in the caliber of DJs. I have much respect for DJs that are driven by a passion to create music that pushes boundaries. DJs who create incredible mixes that take you to someplace you've never experienced. Superstars, producers, niche club DJs, and under-ground DJs with creative talent and mad skill are typically not found performing at weddings. Weddings require someone that will play a broad mix of genres and please the majority of a large mix of people. I can't imagine that a guy like Skrillex (an innovator in the music industry) would enjoy playing a set of 90's country tunes followed by a classic Huey Lewis and B-52's mix... every weekend of the summer. I imagine that his soul would die a little each time he even heard the Macarena. The wedding industry simply does not attract this type of DJ (highly advanced in skill, but plays a narrow selection of genres and usually detests "pop radio tunes").

Wedding DJs, as a group, have a poor reputation in the entertainment industry. This is no guess; it is simply a fact. The reason is simple and it starts with this question: How much talent does it take to push the play button? A person might argue that DJs are not "real" musicians because they're simply playing other people's music. This topic of conversation is best left for another time or a different book. However, it's very important to understand this mindset because it's what separates the stereotypical wedding DJ from the expert entertainers.

There are plenty of reasons why a person may be enticed to become a wedding DJ, and this single question is what brings in those temporary performers that play for a summer and then hang up their headphones after realizing how difficult it actually is. It's the same reason why most don't achieve much success in the industry. They realize, through experience, that it is much harder to please an entire group of diverse demographics for an entire night simply by "pushing play". The simple formula of having a pre-made set list and mixing in song requests will not produce excellent results seen on the dance floor and the length people stay to enjoy the wedding. With the ease of digital media and streaming services, becoming a wedding DJ seems appealing because of the low startup costs and minimal gear required. No longer do you have to lug around cases of records, or cassette tapes, or CDs. Large mixing boards seem to be a thing of the past. It is not a mystery as to why this industry attracts a large amount of inexperienced or untrained DJs.

So what happens is that when people go to multiple weddings in a season, they may see five subpar wedding DJs and maybe one good or great DJ. And that good or great DJ might not have even been trained in skills such as power mixing, scratching, beat matching, and/or mixing in key. Wedding guests end up lowering their expectations and can get to the point where they dread going to weddings because they know what to expect - the same one hundred songs they hear at every wedding, being played too loud by a DJ that won't take their song requests. This is why we don't get much respect from the rest of the entertainment industry. But the shiny golden nugget that we can take away from this is that if you are a hard-working and dedicated performer, then you will easily standout from your competition.

Why people still end up with subpar wedding DJs

1) The subpar DJ is inexpensive. When a bride sets her budget and starts shopping around, she may quickly realize that a wedding costs much more than she anticipated. If she asks a reputable wedding DJ how much they cost, quite often they get sticker shocked by their cost and shop around until they find someone that fits their budget.

2) The bride and groom decide to put more money from their budget into other services such as photography, catering, or decorations. This leaves them with hiring the cheapest DJ they can find, which usually ends up being an amateur or rookie with little experience.

3) The bride and groom waited too long to book their entertainment. Great wedding DJs typically book their weekend weddings a year or two in advance. Last-minute bookings leave them with little to no other options.

4) They don't realize or don't care that there are better DJs out there. All of their friends just got married and they all hired the same guy who played the exact same music at each wedding. They all had a good time and they hope to have a

good time too. Too bad all the other guests at those weddings didn't have as good of time.

5) Large companies sometimes do a bait-and-switch. This is where they have a star DJ on their roster that the bride thinks she booked, but at the last moment, the star DJ has to go do a higher-paying gig (they usually make up some other reason) so she gets left with the high school kid that's being trained this summer.

6) They have a friend who used to DJ. Usually, this is the worst idea ever.

7) The bride and groom believe that all wedding DJs are the same.

You can start to see why the majority of these weddings will end up with a subpar DJ. And it's not just because better DJs cost more money (I know of many DJs that slack off on a regular basis and still charge high rates). The most important reason on the list is the last one. When you start performing at a higher level, people will instantly notice. It makes for easy referrals and your reputation will soon spread.

> **Pro Secret:** Your reputation of consistently delivering high quality performances will earn you higher paying gigs with less money being spent on advertising.

Expectations and the Top 100 Songs

THERE SEEMS to be a certain level of expectation in regards to song selection at weddings. When DJs play the same one hundred songs at every wedding, people start to expect to hear those same one hundred songs at every wedding. Some people may get very excited for these songs (Y.M.C.A. and Brown Eyed Girl), while others may dread them because they always get played at every wedding they go to and they want to hear something different. What happens is that most newly engaged couples will then hire JUST ANY DJ because they think they'll just play the same songs anyway. What they don't realize is that you can take two different DJs, a rookie and an expert, give them the exact same list of songs to play for the evening, and the expert will consistently end up with fuller dance floors, happier wedding guests, and better testimonials from their clients… every single time.

Pro Secret: The majority of wedding guests expect to hear a big chunk of one hundred of the same songs that they hear at other weddings.

This expectation to hear the same one hundred songs at every wedding is very important. In my area that I perform for, people will expect to hear plenty of classic rock and country songs. My list of songs will be different from the songs in your area, but I guarantee that there will be a list of one hundred songs. Make sure you know your list, because it will be a key to having success in your area. Take them and put them in a playlist folder that you can quickly access; it will come in handy at all times. I've added an appendix that lists the top one hundred songs that are popular in my area. I'm willing to bet that many of them will be the same if you live in Canada or US. We'll touch on this point throughout the book.

The Reception Dance is a Play

TRUMAN CAPOTE said, "Life is a moderately good play with a badly written third act." Don't worry, I'm not going to bore you with a literature lesson, but before we get into specific song choices we should take a moment to analyze how a theatrical play is designed, because it is the same way a set list is created to entertain an audience for an entire night.

The dramatic arc has five parts:

1) **Exposition** – This is the back-story, the events before the plot starts to unfold. It tells the setting of the story. For our wedding, we call this cocktail hour and dinner music. It's our chance to lay a foundation of songs that hints at what type of music people can expect to dance to. If

it's a beach themed wedding, then we might throw in some soft romantic tunes by Bob Marley such as Three Little Birds or Turn Your Lights Down Low. This way people won't be surprised when they hear some faster-paced reggae music later on in the night.

2) **Rising Action** – These are the most important parts in a play because they set up the climax and ultimately (in time) the finale. Each event that takes place builds and builds until it gets to the most exciting point of the story (climax). When we DJ weddings (or any party for that matter), we want to slowly build up excitement throughout the night.

Pro Secret: Don't play the most popular songs at the beginning of the dance, save them for the climax and falling action.

3) **Climax** - The climax is the turning point in a story. It is the highest part of the arc where the story starts to unfold. This is the part of the wedding where the real partiers and dancing guests finally get to know the DJ's style. The expert entertainer starts to unfold from the "safe" songs and begins to explore uncon-ventional song choices.

4) **Falling Action** – This is the part of the play where the bad guy and good guy have been chasing each other and finally end up at a big suspenseful moment. For wedding DJs, it's the time right after the midnight lunch leading up to the end of the night.

5) **Denouement** – This literally means the untying of a knot. The conflicts are resolved to make the viewer feel relief from the anxiety buildup. These are the final dances of the night, which I prefer to be an anthem people like singing to when they're drunk, followed by two slow songs or a super popular fast song or a theme song for the bridal party (a song with significant meaning for those involved with the wedding).

We need to keep these five points in mind, as they will shape our entire evening and all the mini set lists that make up the evening. Do not disregard this. It is the main idea behind entertaining for an entire night's party. I cannot stress this enough. It is the winning formula for creating outstanding set lists. Memorize and use it accordingly. From now on we shall refer to this as the Music Arc. Now let us dive into the good stuff.

Building Your Set List(s)

THERE are many things that differentiate the two levels of DJing, including mic work, presentation, mixing skills, participation, quality of equipment, energy levels and more. But I'm only going to focus on song selections and set lists because I feel it is the single biggest improvement a new DJ can make that can be learned the quickest and show immediate results at the next gig they play.

A set list is a group of songs that will be played throughout the evening. Most receptions will last from 5pm until 2am. That's seven hours of dance music, or 140 dance songs that you will play during the evening (the first few hours are cocktail/dinner music). That may appear to be a lot of music, and it can seem daunting if you had to pre-select each and every song and the exact order in which they need to be played in. This is the single biggest flaw for do-it-yourselfers that figure they can just DJ their own wedding by hitting shuffle on their MP3 player. Even just picking 140 songs can be tricky, because you don't know which guests will be attending the wedding and which guests will want to dance and when they'll want to dance. Enter the art of DJing a wedding.

Pro Secret: The final version of your set list will be built while you DJ the wedding in real time.

It is impossible to have the same amount of success at every single wedding every time by playing the exact same songs in the exact same order. Each wedding will be different depending on the amount of guests, demographics of guests, venue, order of events, and preferences of the bridal party. Preparing your entire evening in advance and expecting not to have to tend to your list is very unrealistic if you want to have any success in this business.

It is a great idea, however, to approach each wedding with a game plan that is flexible. We do this by building multiple set lists that will ultimately end up being the evening's entire set list. Building these mini set lists is imperative to having success early on in your DJ career while you learn the ropes. There are many options for how we choose to organize our songs.

Mini Set Lists by Genre

A common method is to group songs into their own genres. However, we need to be more specific than that to make our job easier during the reception. Breaking them into three mini groups of ten songs is the easiest way to grab whichever songs you need in the quickest way possible. Keep things simple by separating songs into these genres:

Oldies (50's 60's 70's)

Rock (80's to current)

Hip/Hop & Rap

Country

Dance/Electronic

Pop

We keep genres simple because we play for a group of people that have a limited knowledge about music. Most people will only recognize songs that they hear on the radio occasionally. The chances are good that they don't even know many musician's names. If I had a dollar for every time a person came up and said something like, "Play the catfish dinner song," when they really mean That's My Kind of Night by Luke Brian, I'd be rich.

Pro Secret: Helping people out by understanding what song they want to hear when they don't know the name of it is a big part of offering great customer service. They will love you if you know what song they are talking about.

Group one will be songs from your top one hundred. Take the ten best songs in a particular genre and slap them in there. Don't worry if you have more than ten songs, just pick the most popular ones. All of these lists will have to be updated regularly, so it will gradually change over time. If you are the nostalgic type or very particular with regards to details, then it's a good idea to write these lists down to save them for later.

Pro Secret: Always update your lists to be current or every three months at the latest.

Group two will be a list of your ten favorite party tunes. The only rule is that these songs must be different than your first group of songs. No repeats allowed. They can be old or new songs as long as they fill up a dance floor or get drinkers singing along. This grouping is your chance to add your style of favorite party tunes that gives you a bit of an identity compared to other DJs.

Group three will be the ten best songs people can dance to. Once again, don't add songs that have shown up in the first two lists. No repeats. For genres like dance and electronic, pick ten dance-floor fillers. For genres like country and rock, pick a mix of 5 dance-floor fillers and 5 slow dances.

Example Mini Set Lists (Country Genre)

Country Top Ten:

Fishing In The Dark – Nitty Gritty Dirt Band

Cadillac Ranch - Nitty Gritty Dirt Band

Guitar Town – Steve Earl

Party For Two – Shania Twain

Up – Shania Twain

Springsteen – Eric Church

That's My Kind Of Night – Luke Bryan

Boot Scootin' Boogie – Brooks and Dunn

Friends In Low Places – Garth Brooks

Wagon Wheel – Darious Rucker

Country Party:

She's With Me – High Valley

Red Solo Cup – Toby Keith

Country Road – Bob Denver

Beer in My Hand – Eric Church

Ticks – Brad Paisley

It's Friday – Dean Brody

Folsom Prison – Johnny Cash

Family Tradition – Hank Williams, Jr.

Something Like That – Tim McGraw

I Love This Bar – Toby Keith

Country Dance:

Mean to Me – Rett Eldrige

Head Over Boots – Jon Pardi

Redneck Woman – Bellamy Brothers

Small Town Saturday Night – Hal Ketchum

Dust on the Bottle – David Lee Murphy

Chattahoochee – Alan Jackson

Honey Bee – Blake Shelton

I Cross My Heart – George Strait

Amarillo By Morning – George Strait

My Wish – Rascal Flats

Mini Set Lists by Mood

If we remember that our reception is like a play, then we will pick our songs based on the current mood of the guests or current feeling of the room and then also consider where we want to take them. If everyone is just chilling out and casually drinking, then it would be a bad idea to crank out a loud beat with a high bpm (fast tempo). We need to guide them there by gradually increasing the tempo or more importantly ramping up the feeling of an intense or high level of fun party. We can label these moods as:

Mello (Laid back and relaxed)

Gearing up (Easy to dance to, warming up the floor)

Romantic (Slow tempo, full of emotion)

Party Groove (100bpm, deep beats and/or fan favorites and anthems)

Party Hard (128 bpm, fun favorites, hot new tunes and old favorites)

Bangers (Full energy, loud and fast)

Build these playlists up with your favorite tunes, hot tracks, and songs off the top 100 list. These lists should contain around 25 songs each.

Pro Secret: DJing is all about creating feelings and moods. Get good at recognizing what mood people are in to know where start and have a realistic goal for where you want to take them.

Mini Set Lists By Decades

Organizing some of your favorite tracks by decades is a great way to be ready for any crowd. I've played some weddings that really love the 50's and 60's, so much so that it was pretty much all I played all night. Other weddings will have a flow of different age groups that come and go. Children love the hot new songs, 30 year olds love the music they partied to in high school or college (90's), older parents may really love the 70's. When you get that core group on the floor, sometimes playing a group of songs from the same era will keep them out dancing longer.

Music acts as a hypnotic anchor. When people experience important events, they attach the songs they were listening to at that time to those events. Whenever they hear the song, it immediately takes them back to that happy memory (example: first kiss). Coming of age (15-21 years) is when people will create the most hypnotic anchors in their life because they experience a large amount of important life events. The music during that time always lives with them and holds a special place in their heart. So if you can figure out the general age group you're playing for, do some quick math to correlate the decade they lived in when they were 20 years old, this will tell you what chunk of songs will be most appealing to them. The unique thing about hypnotic anchors is that it can be absolutely any song for absolutely any reason and which makes it hard for us DJs to guess which songs will immediately spark those happy memories with some people. Perhaps the theme song to "Fresh Prince of Bel Air" will be the winner or maybe everyone was listening to Def Leppard at their high school parties. This is where investigating the background of your wedding party will provide big dividends out on the dance floor later in the night. I'm not suggesting you hire a private detective, but a simple question to the Best Man such as "What songs do you guys drink beer to in college" might suffice.

Pro Secret: Songs become hypnotic anchors when they are attached to highly emotional memories.

Mini Set Lists by Events

I believe that an important part of DJing weddings is having a go-to set list for every part of a wedding, including the ceremony. Make sure to include enough songs to fill in the set amount of time for each event:

Pre-Ceremony traditional (1 hour): Classic wedding instrumental music.

Pre- Ceremony contemporary (1 hour): Relaxing and romantic songs for this decade, mix of instrumentals and vocals.

Ceremony: Specific songs picked by the bride and groom for the processional, recessional, registry signing and any other special event.

Post-Ceremony (1 hour): Classic love songs from all decades with a lighter and more upbeat feeling.

Cocktails (1 hour): Laid-back music with a happier upbeat tempo. Nothing that will put you to sleep, but music that makes a person want to hang out and converse with old friends over a beer.

Dinner music (1.5 hours): Quieter, romantic music, nothing loud and obnoxious. People want to be able to comfortably talk. Should be a mix of old with plenty of new. Slowly sets the stage for the night to come (exposition).

Special dances: Song choices from bride and groom including (but not limited to) the grand entrance, first dance, wedding party, father/daughter, mother/son, cake cutting, bouquet toss, garter belt, and last dance of the night.

Dance games/Icebreakers: Your favorite songs that get people up on the floor by way of game or other gimmick. Example: Longevity dance – It Must Be Love by Alan Jackson.

Line dances: This can be very area sensitive, but typically include the most popular line dances and special dance move songs. Example: Watch Me (Whip/Nae Nae), Y.M.C.A., Cha Cha Slide, etc.

Midnight lunch: All weddings will reach a midnight lunch point. It's a good idea to have a pre-made list to back you up in case you need to grab a quick bite to eat and have to leave your booth.

Set-up (2 hours): A mix of your own favorite songs to listen to while you set up your equipment for the gig.

Take-down (2 hours): After the dance is done, a good mix of chill music to mellow out the hard partiers.

Drive home (2 hours): A mobile DJ always has a drive home. Have a list of songs ready to listen to so that you don't get distracted picking out your songs while you drive.

Mini Set Lists by Top 40

Top 40 songs are the most popular songs at any given time. There are many different top 40 lists, but most songs that gain massive popularity will show up on multiple top 40 lists. I prefer America Top 40 with Ryan Seacrest and Billboard for my top 40 lists because it most closely represents the type of music my typical crowds will have listened to.

Create a new top 40 list every three months and hold onto all your past lists for easy reference. The typical crowd of wedding guests will be a little slower when it comes to recognizing which songs are popular or familiar to them. Music lovers will always be searching for the next popular song before it comes out, music fans will always be up to date with the hottest tracks, but your average wedding guest pulls from the top 40 list that happened three months ago. If you are performing at a wedding in June, then your best bet is to look at the top 40 list from March or April.

DJ Performance Set List

If you are a skilled DJ then I probably don't have to even mention this set list. For the aspiring rookies though, this is the list of songs you will use to perform a mashup or scratch set.

Pro Secret: All DJs are entertainers. People are always watching you and can be entertained (even amazed) by watching you perform a mash up or scratch set. (Kid Rock would always put on a show of scratching records and drinking Jim Beam while smoking cigs… hardcore partier? You bet, but very entertaining.) I highly encourage all DJs to take a mixing course to learn this incredible art.

Where to Find Songs

NOW THAT you know what type of set lists you need to create before you show up to your wedding gig, you will need to fill them up with songs. This can be extremely difficult if you simply try to recall them all from memory. There is no shame in researching and pulling ideas from lists posted online. The internet has a plethora of lists available including Billboard's Hot 100 or America Top 40, but there are more ways to find the songs you need.

Collecting specific songs for your area is a great way to gain instant credibility with the locals. Go out to pubs, bars, clubs and dances to hear what people are listening to on a regular basis. Listen to all different types of radio stations in your area, not just your favorite one. Check out streaming service websites including Spotify, Apple Music (iTunes), and IHeartRadio. Sometimes you can even find lists of songs that get played on the satellite radio channels. Music video channels such as Much Music or MTV will constantly update their top hits list.

Compilation albums are quick ways to gather the most popular songs of a particular year. Most genres will have their own series which makes it even easier to sort out in your song database. Big Shiny Tunes, Now, Country Heat, Ultra Dance, Groove Station, and Grammy Nominees are some great examples of compilation albums. Greatest hits albums of specific musicians can be another great way to collect a large amount of songs in a hurry.

Sometimes the bride and groom may be big fans of a local band that has original songs. You can score big points if you get your hands on these tracks. I've even had grooms that are in bands and play a set with their bandmates during the wedding. Having songs that are similar to their band's set list are handy to have when you need to follow up after their performance.

Pro Secret: Big-name bands on tour get people excited. Play songs from artists that have just recently performed or will be coming to perform soon. It's always my go-to trick to get people excited.

Asking the bride and groom the following questions will help you nail down what songs you need to have ready on the wedding night:

What year did you graduate high school? (Finding the biggest hits from that year are usually winners.)

Do you have any favorite movies or TV shows? (Movies always have recognizable music that, if played at the right time, can really hit a home run with the newlyweds.)

What are the bride's favorite songs/bands/genres?

What are the groom's favorite songs/bands/genres?

Do their parents have a special song from their wedding that they would like to hear again?

What songs are on your DO NOT PLAY list? (It's very important that if you ask this, then you adhere to it.)

Pro Secret: Professional sport teams may have certain songs as their anthems. Their intro song on game days are popular choices for grand entrances for the sport fan bride & grooms.

Another great way to collect a list of songs is by writing down each and every song request at the weddings and gigs you play for. You will always get an eclectic assortment of songs you've never heard before. Sometimes it feels like guests are playing a game with themselves called "stump the DJ". Write these songs down and then the next day, listen to them before you buy them. Some of them may be garbage you will never play, so don't waste your money on everything. One time at a grade 8 dance a kid requested a clean version of a Wu-Tang Clang song. I don't think those tracks exist, but if they did, I still wouldn't play them. That would be like eating macaroni and cheese with no cheese… it's just not right.

Movies always have recognizable music that, if played at the right time, can really hit a home run with the newly-weds. Keeping in touch with pop culture is a huge factor in what separates great DJs from mediocre ones. I personally know many DJs in their 50's that are still rocking young parties because they keep up with the times. Knowing what movies are popular with each age group is an excellent way to create instant rapport with your crowd. For example, when Night at the Roxbury came out in 1998, it made the song "What is Love by Haddaway" even more popular than when it was initially released in 1993. In 2011, A Thousand Years was one of the most popular bridal songs not just because it's a great song, but because it's attached to The Twilight Saga which was one of the most successful Young Adult film series ever. You can almost expect that when these 15 year old girls grow up and get married when they are 30 years old (in the year 2026) that this song will be a possibility that has slipped their mind but could be a real winner for them if you suggest it.

Children's movie soundtracks will always be a great place to get popular songs for the youngest of guests. Often times, a hit animated movie will utilize a great track from the past and the kids will immediately recognize it when it's played. When Shrek 2 was released, it crushed the box office with kids coming out in droves to see it. The main song the kids remembered from it was Funkytown by Lipps, Inc. Still to this day, if I ever play it, children that have seen the movie will rush to the dance floor. This was the same for Happy – Pharrell Williams from Despicable Me 2 and also Can't Stop The Feeling – Justin Timberlake from Trolls.

You can also ask your DJ community what works for them. Some DJs can be greedy and overly protective about killer tracks they've found and use, but I've found that if I share my experiences with most DJs, then they will typically share their findings back with me and then eventually the whole DJ community benefits from it in the end.

Once you've acquired a new track, make sure to tag it with information so you can organize it better and find it easier. Typical metadata to include can be; artist, title, genre, BPM, key, and mood. If your program has a comment section for each track, then add any other info here. I like to list which songs it pairs well or mixes well with, before and after.

Place these new tracks into a folder to listen to. When we download multiple tracks at a time, we can forget about which great songs we've added and end up not listening to them and eventually, forgetting about them because they get lost in our database/library. I label this folder as "New" (if they are recent releases) "Old" (if they are older releases that you've never listened to) or "Listen To" (if you want to group them all into one folder.) Most songs will live in this folder until I'm comfortable with all the beats and truly know the song (usually takes around 30 listens.) It is important to truly know and understand what tracks you have so that you can recall them at a later date. There is nothing worse than not being able to remember "that one song" or even to have completely forgotten about it.

50,000 Song Library

A COMMON MARKETING ploy amongst DJ companies is to advertise that they have a huge song library. This was another way of saying; we have every song that you could possibly want to listen to at your wedding. It may have been very important back when people lugged vinyl, or cassettes, or even CDs to every event, but now we have access to the internet. Most DJs will be able to access any song at any time. It has come to the point where it is almost expected by the majority of the younger audience! But even if you did have a 50,000 song library, how many of those songs would actually play well for a wedding dance? If you were to hit shuffle on this entire library, I'm willing to bet that you would be compelled to skip a great number of songs because you simply don't want to hear it. Now consider if anyone would even want to dance to the majority of those songs. For any new DJ that feels they simply do not have a big enough collection of music they can access, I want them to consider this statement: "Weddings only have time to play a set number of dance songs ranging from 100 to 200 songs during the event."

Due to the limited amount of time you have, you'll have to play only the best songs to get people dancing. A DJ does not have time or any good excuse to play a song that they feel is mediocre at best unless it is a high priority and specific song request. Even if you were to include song requests, you may only get 30 requests at the most, which is where you may run into the problem of not having a particular song. But this can be avoided, for the most part, by doing your meetings with the wedding couple before hand, ensuring that you will bring with you all the songs that *they* want to hear. So if you are new to the DJ game and you don't have a large list of songs, then either make sure you can access the internet during the event or do your homework with the wedding couple and also have the songs from the top 100 list to get you through the first couple of gigs.

Pro Secret: You do not need a massive song library to be a very successful wedding DJ.

Putting it All Together

YOU'VE DONE your homework. You've found all the songs you need for the night and have organized them into their set lists. You've just finished setting up and the first batch of wedding guests are arriving at the venue.

5pm – Cocktail Hour

This is the exposition. It is very important that you lay the groundwork of what the guests should expect to hear throughout the night. The volume should be very low and monitored as more and more people fill up the venue. Constantly perform a sound check by walking to different areas of the venue listening to the level of volume, highs and lows, and ensuring you can easily carry on a conversion with someone. If anyone has to yell or raise their voice to talk, then it's not at a comfortable volume level. You have plenty of party time to crank it up, so just relax and play it chill for now.

6pm – Grand Entrance

Play the song the bride and groom picked out. It should be at a louder level, but not so loud that children and geriatrics are covering their ears. This is typically a "pump up" song that sets the tone and says, "We're ready to get the party started tonight!" It can also be a very romantic song for classy receptions.

6:15pm – Dinner Music

Relaxed and chill music at a very low level so that people can comfortably talk while they eat.

Pro Secret: The number one complaint about DJs at weddings is that they play their music too loud. Keep your volume in check and leave lots of room to crank it up for when the party is ready to explode!

7:30pm – First Dance (special dances)

Volume should be at 70% of your dance night level. Leave room for the volume to be turned up and slowly introduce the fact that this party will be in full swing soon.

7:45pm – Open Dancing

Pro Secret: Only play genres for 15 - 25 min at a time. Five song limit, then switch to a new genre.

The first song of the night will be important to set the tone. It lets people know what they can expect for the rest of the night - a fun party!!! People have been sitting for the majority of the night so far, some have already had enough alcoholic drinks, and other guests may already be bored with talking to the people at their table. The wedding guests are primed and ready to dance. If the wedding has an abundance of children (3yrs-10yrs), then your best bet is to play a newer pop tune that the kids will love to dance to. They will rush the dance floor and their parents will follow. It will also bring out the group of girls that will be on the floor all night long. The other option is to play a generic "celebration" song, which is less creative and less original, but a safe bet if you're new to the wedding DJ game. See appendix for examples.

An important note to mention here is that there will be a big difference in the number of people dancing early in the night depending on when most people show up. Most weddings will start cocktails at 5pm and feed all their guests, do speeches, and then hit up the dance floor. But occasionally, some brides and grooms will choose to have a small private supper and then invite the majority of the guests for the remainder of the evening, with cocktails starting at 7:00pm and speeches at 7:30pm. From a DJ's perspective, this is setting up an empty dance floor for the night. What happens is that the guests show up at 7:20pm (they're never early or on time) and immediately sit down and have to be quiet to listen to the speeches. Finally, after speeches wrap up at 8:30pm they will grab a round of drinks and socialize with people they haven't seen in a long time. Other people won't even think of hitting the dance floor until they're got enough dancing juice (alcohol) in their system. This usually takes a few hours, which ends up being right around midnight lunch time. So for another 30-45 minutes, people will sit and eat. Finally, by midnight, people will actually be ready and willing to get up and dance.

Pro Secret: If the majority of weddings guests are not invited for the supper, then utilize DJ games to really encourage the guests to get up and dance.

After you've gotten past the first few songs, you should be able to recognize which demographic will want to be dancing and you should cater to that group to start with. The common types of dance groups:

Girl Circles - Usually 3 to 5 five girls that stand in circle and dance with each other to pop songs and top hits. At clubs, they're the ones who put their purses in the middle and dance around them as if they are worshipping them, all the while trying to block out any guy that will interfere with their girl's night out. Ages can be anywhere from 15yrs to late 30's. You gotta love these girls for helping to fill the dance floor, because they will be out there all night long, as long as you play "new" music and top hits. They will lure the drunk guys to the dance floor around midnight. They will only break up their circle during slow songs or expand their circle when oldie anthems come on (Mony Mony, Love Shack, etc.).

Old & New Romantics - These are married couples that actually know how to dance. I love these couples, because as long as you play a song they can dance to (two-step, waltz, etc.) they will dance to it, even if they've never heard the song before. If they can recognize the beat within the first 20 seconds, they will dance to it. If you have at least three of these couple dancing early in the night, then you should focus on catering to them because they will draw out other couples in droves.

Studio Dancers - They've studied ballet, jazz, tap, hip-hop, etc. and can't wait to hear the song that they have choreographed moves to. This also includes young kids that learnt specific dance moves in their school Phys-Ed class. If you haven't played their song in the first two hours, then they will rush your booth in groups and ask you to play those specific songs. Make sure you play those songs from start to finish or you will end up with some very disappointed dancers. Usually appear in groups of 3 or 4 people.

Hopeless Romantics - They've got two left feet and have no sense of rhythm, but will be out on the floor all night long if their love interest is out there too. Usually, they only show up after they're intoxicated, so give them time to hit up the bar. The easiest way to lure them out to the floor is with line dances. They will jump in next to someone who knows the moves and will bumble their way through it, but this is usually enough to keep them out there for a few more songs. I always play a slow dance song before they choose to run away because it will keep them out there for three more songs.

Clubbers - They won't see the dance floor until midnight. Too busy B.S.ing and drinking copious amounts of alcohol, they'll come out for the dance/electronic/hip-hop tunes and the occasional throwback 80's/90's mix. When they finally hit the dance floor, it will immediately ramp up the energy levels and you should roll with it. You can get a solid 30-45 minutes from this group. You will visually be able to see them get exhausted from ridiculous dance moves and can almost hear them thinking about rushing the bar for a round of shots. If you can end the dance set with a newer romantic song (Ed Sheeran or Keith Urban), then they will return to the floor quicker for another round of fun.

Non-Dancers - You won't see these people all night except for the odd dance game where they get peer pressured into taking the dance floor. This is my biggest complaint about dance games; it makes people feel uncomfortable, which is the opposite of what the DJ is supposed to do.

> **Pro Secret**: A great number of people love to just sit and socialize while listening to music. They appreciate it just as much as the dancers, so don't discount them. Entertaining at weddings includes catering to everybody, not just the dancers.

OK. We've labeled our basic dance groups and which genres they like to listen to. Each wedding will have a different number of people in these groups, which is why you can never play the same set list(s) for every wedding you perform at. I've done some weddings where they only wanted to listen to country music. I've done other weddings that only wanted 50's and 60's music. So, if we use the rule of thumb that we'll only play 5 songs max per genre, then how are we supposed to cater to all the different groups of dancers? This is where researching and knowing your sub-genres is very important.

Examples of country music sub-genres; Bluegrass, Classic Country, Country Blues, Country Folk, Country Rap, Stadium Country, Alternative Country, Honky Tonk, Outlaw Country, Western Swing, etc.

Mixing up these styles of music will appeal to the wide range of guests, including the Willie Nelson fans to the Eric Church partiers.

Pro Secret – DJing is 98% preparing and 2% performing.

It's important to note that we should pace ourselves in the song popularity category. We don't want to play all the "good" or "popular" songs at the beginning of the night. Some club DJs may do this because they get a different crowd coming in the door later in the night and they'll just play the hit song a second time. But our crowd is with us for the entire night. The best tactic is to pick a couple of songs on the current month's top 40 list (check out Billboard or another current music chart) and play the ones that appeal to the young children. These are usually the overproduced glam pop stars such as Katy

Perry or Megan Trainor. The kids will enjoy it and won't bug you later in the night, and most of the adults are not dancing yet anyways. We can pace ourselves and play the awesome top 40 songs when the Clubbers hit the floor later in the night. Just ensure that you gradually sneak some in once in a while so they know to stick around. If you were to save ALL the popular songs until after midnight, there may not be anyone around to enjoy them. From my area, there was an old DJ named Top 40 Gordy. He got to the point in his career where he wasn't comfortable with the newer music coming out and eventually stopped updating his playlists. Top 40 Gordy didn't have any of the Top 40 songs. Pretty soon, his phone wasn't ringing anymore and he eventually hung up his headphones. It's very important to stay with the times.

When we consider all the guests at the wedding, we're looking at a very wide age range. It is important to accommodate all ages to ensure everyone has a great time. We cater to the very young children early in the night because they usually leave or fall asleep first. This is the same for the most elderly people at the dance too. We should be playing a few tracks early in the night for them as well because they tend to leave before midnight. If you sprinkle in some old-time waltzes earlier in the night, they will get up to dance and be very appreciative that you included them in the party. They may be very happy to only dance to one or two songs and then sit back for the rest of the night to watch the youth enjoy themselves. So, we should aim to play these songs before midnight lunch. Making additional playlists for "Children" and "Elders" may help you out in a time of need.

As we play our genre sets, we want to consider the energy levels of our dancers. It is unrealistic that our dancers will dance to twenty fast-paced songs in a row. This is not a rave or a nightclub. Imagine how you might feel after you've just done a few fast-paced Irish Jigs. I'd be sucking wind and trying to catch my breath. The best strategy to use is to play a few fast songs, a slow dance, and then bring it back up with a faster (medium or fast) dance.

Example: *Country Music Set*

Guitars, Cadillacs – Dwight Yokam 173bpm (Key of C Major)

Chattahoochi – Alan Jackson 175bpm (Key of C Major)

Two People Fell In Love – Brad Paisley 80bpm (Key of C Major)

Guitar Town – Steve Earl 167bpm (Key of G Major)

The Country Music Set above is an example that works very well for multiple reasons. We've incorporated songs from the top 100 list, Country Dance list, mixed new songs with old songs, and paired up the first two songs with the same bpm and key. Guitars, Cadillacs can be mixed seamlessly with Chattahoochi because they're both in the key of C Major (it will sound like a professional mix), and because they are the same tempo (174bpm after you sync them up) the two-steppers on the floor can keep dancing at the exact same speed without missing a beat or having to adjust to a new speed. Slowing down to 80bpm will be a perfect time for them to catch their breath, and once again, it's a song in the key of C Major. Next, if we were using the Camelot Wheel (found on Harmonic-Mixing.com) we would read that a song in the key of C Major can be mixed with a new song in the key of G Major. If you listen to Two People and Guitar Town, it will sound like those two songs are brothers. If you are unfamiliar with beat matching and harmonic mixing, then I strongly recommend that you research and learn these two techniques immediately. They will dramatically improve your sets and change the way you consider mixing music. These two techniques are so important because they produce a soothing feeling to the mind. Subconsciously, we get a feeling that these songs belong together. We know something sounds great together, but oftentimes the average person will not be able to distinguish what just happened. It's a very sneaky way for DJs to put together more successful sets that the dancers will enjoy. With today's technology, it is very easy to find and label tempo and key for every song. If your software does not do it automatically, then I suggest that you take the time to label or tag your tracks using info found on websites such as songbpm.com and notediscover.com.

Pro Secret – Harmonic mixing using the Camelot System is often more important than tempo matching.

Don't constrain yourself exclusively to beat matching and key mixing, because it may limit your set list or you may miss what's happening on the dance floor. Most new DJs forget to look up and see what's going on. At any given time during the night, I'll have three different possible songs I can switch to depending on what happens during the current song. You need to be able to quickly adapt to any sudden changes. Hone your ninja-like skills to be able to adapt to any situation on the fly. A common thing that may happen is that you play a few songs that get the crowd geared up. You read this energy level reaction and quickly plan your next three songs to play because you want to ramp up the party. But then all of a sudden a Girl Circle girl comes running to the booth to request a song. 99% of the time, this song will have significant meaning to that Girl Circle. Instead of sticking to your next 3 songs you had planned out, you need to have the confidence to dump that idea and quickly load up that requested song because it is sure to be a killer. Even if it doesn't fit with your beat matching or tempo mixing, go with your gut instinct. This is probably the biggest reason and advantage for having all of your music downloaded onto your device instead of using a streaming service. It's too difficult to pull up a song in less than five seconds if it's not already on your hard-drive. I don't stream music for the biggest reason being I'm usually DJing in a metal curling rink in a small town with no Wi-Fi and terrible reception. In the event that you don't have that song, just be honest and tell that person you don't have it immediately. Write it down and try purchasing it so that it can be played later in the night after it's fully downloaded.

Pro Secret – Timing is everything. You need to play the right song at the right time.

Switching between genres can also pose a problem for some people. There is, most definitely, a right way and wrong way to approach this. Your biggest clues as to which genre to switch to, will be the age of the dancers on the floor, how long they've been dancing for, and the time of the night. If there has been a majority of older folks on the floor dancing to a county set and then an oldies set, they may very well be ready to sit down and take a break. Depending on the demographic of the newcomers to the floor, you'll be able to get a read on what to switch to. If, for example, there is an influx of young children, then switching to a current top 40 pop set will be your best choice. Or if there happens to be a group of Clubbers and it's later in the evening, switching to a 90's Hip-Hop set could be the winner.

At the end of your genre set, let the last song play all the way to the end. This will be the perfect time to grab the mic and make an announcement to give a solid break in music. It acts as a buffer from one song to the next. If you were to play a romantic song and then instantly switch to a hard hitting rock/metal song, you will destroy flow and start to turn people off. It leaves them feeling confused and results in an empty dance floor. If there is no need for a break or if you feel that a small break in music will wreck the vibe, then you will want to search for a song that is a genre mix. Often times artists from two separate genres will collaborate on a song which makes it easy for us DJs to maintain a flow. Pitbull is actually a big country music fan. He has done collaborations with musicians such as Tim McGraw and even Keith Urban (Sun Don't Let Me Down). This makes sense considering Keith Urban's style of country can be described as Stadium Country. It fills stadiums with young partiers who often also like hip-hop or pop. If we played Sun Don't Let Me Down with Urban and Pitbull (108 bpm) we could mix into Pitbull's Fun (114 bpm). Going in the other direction, you may have a dance song such as Wake Me Up – Avicii. It features an acoustic guitar throughout the song and has been covered by Country musicians Tebey with Emerson Drive. Keep your eyes out for cover tunes across genres. There are plenty of songs out there and will come in handy when you need them in a pinch (put them all together in their own folder for easy searching).

Open Dancing will also be broken up by various wedding events. If at all possible, convince the wedding couple to stagger everything in 30-minute or one-hour increments.

7:45pm – Special dances

8:30pm – Play two different genre sets

9:00pm – Cake cutting, then play four more genre sets

10:00pm – Bouquet toss and garter belt, then play four more genre sets

11:00pm – Midnight lunch set

11:30pm – Party set with multiple genres

1:30pm – Last call

1:55pm – Last dance

11:00pm – Midnight Lunch Set

Decrease the volume level from open dancing level to a reasonable level where people can converse. This is a great time to play the ever-growing list of requested songs that are not good dance choices (because everyone will be eating instead of dancing anyways). It can also be the best time to play new hot dance songs that have a slower beat of around 100bpm. In 2016, my go-to list included Drake, Justin Bieber, Major Lazer and The Chainsmokers. It was a great way to say to all the younger guests, "Don't leave for the club, because we're getting ready to crank up the music." This is also the time when a lot of older folks are considering packing it in for the night and most young children have fallen asleep under the tables. It's the perfect time to approach Climax and enter Falling Action, when the drunk clubbers will fill the dance floor with the wedding party. The content of the music will also start to loosen up. I play very clean content with no explicit words or lyrics before 11:00pm and then slowly loosen up as the night gets later, depending on who is still at the wedding. Always check with the bride, groom, and their parents if you are concerned about content restrictions. Wedding groups can be very liberal and others can be very conservative. Know your audience,

1:30am – Last Call Set

Finally, we've reached the end of the Falling Action and we're entering the Denouement. If you've paced yourself appropriately and followed the mood on the dance floor, you should be able to play pretty much anything and they'll eat it up. But it's not a time to slack off and take the easy route. Keep pushing to find the best songs each and every time. When it's announced that it is last call for alcohol sales, some people may rush the bar and load up on lots of drinks. Sometimes a drinking anthem such as Shots – LMFAO or Drink – Lil Jon will ramp the energy level up through the roof. One time at a late-night wedding, last call was given and the bridal party whipped out 5 bottles of champagne that they had forgotten about. In their intoxicated state, they struggled to get them open. This gave me enough time to load up Champagne Showers – LMFAO. The timing was so perfect that they lost their minds when they popped them open and shook 'em up to spray some bubbly over the entire venue. I was cleaning my speakers for a good hour afterwards. It's a good idea to put a clause in your contract that they will be charged an additional fee if this type of thing happens.

As DJs, we have a certain level of responsibility when it comes to crowd control. It's our job to get the party going, but if it gets out of hand, we need to do our best to scale it down or shut it down in a hurry. We don't want to end up like Limp Bizkit playing Break Stuff at Woodstock. The venue owners will appreciate it and so will the bride and groom if they have their name on all the contracts. So, please use discretion at every party you perform at.

Last call is a perfect time to be playing sing-along anthems such as Friends In Low Places by Garth Brooks or Hooked on a Feeling by Blue Swede. Creating a bonding moment for the wedding party is a great way to anchor positive memories for everyone at the party. It's a great way to end the night and get potential bookings because people will tend to latch on to these emotionally high times and remember the good parts of the night, and if you're lucky, correlate it to that great DJ that had the party pumping.

Before you reach the last song of the night, make sure to play at least two slow songs. I prefer to play one really romantic one (for the ones in a relationship already) and one for the couples that are hooking up that night. The two slow songs theory works like this. People already know that time for a dance is running out. This can be reinforced by doing a shout-out thanking the bride and groom for having you perform at their wedding. A sense of urgency is put into the minds of the people that want to connect with a new fling. When you play the first slow song, if you're lucky, these people will hook up for that romantic dance. But chances are pretty good that both of them are not on the dance floor at the same time. When the first song starts to wrap up, everyone that wanted to have that last special dance takes notice of what is happening and tries to rush out to catch the last 30 seconds of the song, or they miss it entirely and are left feeling like they missed their big chance. Adding that second slow song gives everyone hope and a chance to redeem themselves, and they will thank you for it (sometimes they'll even come up to tell you personally). Plus, some girls have a tough time getting their "men" to dance, so once they've got them, they don't want to let them go.

> **Pro Secret:** Always play two slow songs in a row before you play your last song of the night.

1:55pm Last Song

If the last song of the night has not been chosen by the bride and groom, then it leaves some opportunity to create a lasting memory. You can either play a signature closing song that you play at every dance (Ex: Not Ready to Go – The Trews), or ride the wave with what has worked best throughout the night and play an upbeat song with big breaks and drops (Ex: Give Me Everything – Pitbull), or go the sentimental route (We Can't Stop – Miley Cyrus or We Are Young – FUN). You will know if you've done your job properly by hearing them chant "One more song!" Just remember not to play that extra song unless you're getting paid for it and it's okay with the venue manager. Always leave them wanting more.

2:00pm Clean Up

It's okay to play music during your cleanup. The bar staff will appreciate it and it makes our jobs as DJs more relaxing after a hard night's work. But before you hit random auto play on your cleanup set list, give a few minutes of silence to let everyone know that the DJ is done. I usually wait until the lights get turned back on and have one of my speakers shut off.

Pro Secret: Even though the dance party is done, you're still on the job representing your company. Be sure that your cleanup music is not offensive or reputation damaging.

Chicken or the Egg?

WHAT CAME FIRST? The chicken or the egg? This question relates to the problem of how to get a specific group of dancers to the floor. Do we attract people to the floor by playing their specific type of music or do we play their favorite type of music after they've finally come to the dance floor. I believe the answer is a little bit of both.

If we are playing a wedding with a lot of active romantics that have been dancing all night long to two stepping songs or waltzes, then the chances are pretty good that the clubbers are going to stay away from the dance floor. Two things can happen; they'll either get fed up because you're not playing any of their music, or else they'll come right up to you and request that you play their style of music instead. The tricky thing that can happen is once you start to switch gears, the romantics will be upset that you're not playing their songs anymore. They will be even more upset if no one else is going out to the dance floor after you've switched genres/moods. Switching from Jazz or Country into EDM could be a bad idea because they are so very opposite of each other in terms of mood. It would be best to gradually phase one style out with a mix of the newer style. The theory being that you can keep at least half of the romantics dancing while attracting half of the clubbers.

Switching over to bangin' club style music will not always automatically make the ballers pop out of their seats to start raving. If they're drinking heavy, they may be working on one or two drinks that they'll want to finish before hitting the floor. Or if they're socializing, they may be in the middle of a great story that takes another 15 minutes to finish up. Whatever the reason may be, it's going to take some time for the majority of them to take notice and respond. It's our job to "prime" them up and gradually convince them to hit the floor. Sometimes throwing in a throwback set (80's or 90's) can offer a good mix for both the current dancers and future dancers. Line dances or specialty dances can be excellent options to transition over as well.

The clubbers that have had enough drinks or socializing for the night, may just decide to rush the dance floor regardless of what type of music is on. This is your cue to switch over to that pumpin' dance music to start ramping up the mood. But once again, do it with a gradual transition. Keep the flow and control the mood to gain maximum effect. If done properly, you can keep the old and new romantic dancers out on the floor to partake in the aggressive club style music. Everyone likes to feel included and people love to feel young again. There's something memorable about seeing an 80 year old grooving to the latest Pitbull song and actually pulling it off (not looking awkward while doing it.)

If you are dealing with an empty dance floor, then it is clear that you get to choose the music that will bring out the dancers. If it is empty and a group rushes your booth to ask for a specific genre, then it is very clear to roll with their request.

> **Pro Secret:** DJing is rarely black and white. Most situations are in a grey area that requires flexibility. Keep an open mind to new situations that arise and if you can adapt and learn, then your skill level will grow.

Handling Requests

TAKING SONG REQUESTS can be deal breaker for some bride and grooms. If you don't take requests, they may not hire you. I believe it is in the DJ's best interest to take song requests from wedding guests. There are many benefits to accepting song requests. Brides and grooms love this option because it makes them feel that their wedding will be more personalized for them throughout the night. It does not matter how many forms or questionnaires you give them to fill in before the wedding, there is simply no way of knowing which songs they will want to hear on the night of their wedding. It does not matter how many times you sit down to talk with them before the wedding, I can almost guarantee you that they will come up to ask for a different song. Make sure you play every song they request.

Pro Secret: When someone requests a song that you will play, make sure they are in the room to hear it.

People will often requests songs that do not immediately fit within the genre set you are playing. Unless it's coming from someone very important or unless the song is a perfect fit, DO NOT interrupt a flowing set of music to play their instant request. You should get anywhere between ten and forty song requests in a night. On the flip side, do not wait too long to play their requests or the guest might get irritated. But look for the best possible place to insert the song amongst your genre sets. Often times a certain requested song that you feel will not go over well, will go over very well if it has a special meaning to many members in the family. So don't instantly judge a song, just because you don't personally like it. But I will reiterate the exception of immediately playing requests if it comes directly from the Bride or Groom. If they come up to ask for a song, it's because they want to hear it. Always check with them if they would like it played immediately or to wait until a certain guest returns. Playing their requested song at the wrong time can be just as bad as not playing it at all.

If you end up getting a bunch of stinker song requests, you can save them up during midnight lunch and play them all at once. , I will announce it. "I have a bunch of song requests that I will play not". This may seem like a

Get-Out –Of-Jail-Free card, but it's still on you because you're playing them. People can be very judgmental and think that every song a DJ plays was his choice. They are true to a certain extent. As a DJ, you don't have to play every single song that gets requested. I have personally talked down songs that are too vulgar to be played at any wedding and instead made a suggestion to a song that is similar but less offensive. If someone requested you to play Sic – Slipknot, you'd probably get lots of glares and lose potential further gigs. It's very important to protect your reputation, so don't let every single song request dictate what you play.

Pro Secret: When a song is requested that I don't personally like, I will announce it as "Going out by request." It will save a bit of your reputation if other people agree that a song stinks, but will understand that you're doing your job to play requested songs.

If you don't have the song a person requested, then tell them you don't have it and write it down so you can acquire it the next day and have it ready for your next performance. In fact, you should write down absolutely every request because sometimes it can get busy and you may forget. Writing down requested songs in front of the person that requested it also shows that you care about them. It shows them that you've listened and understood them. This is a big part of customer service as a mobile

DJ and will gain you positive reputation points with the crowd. At the end of the night, you will have a list of songs that have been requested that you can use to your advantage. The next day, you will be able to acquire the songs you didn't have and reflect on which songs were very popular.

Pro Secret: The day after a performance is the best time to update playlists and acquire new songs. It is still fresh in your head and you've had some to time to reflect on what worked and what didn't work.

If you have some songs that you absolutely refuse to play, then be prepared to tell the requester that. Never ever lie. Never say you`ll play it and "accidently" forget. You'll get bad reputation in a hurry. Instead, just be honest. People may not like it, but they will respect it. I always refuse to play I'm Too Sexy – Right Said Fred (so the girls can surround the groom and take his clothes off) unless the Bride and Groom absolutely want it. Personally, I think it's creepy when Aunt Velma is taking cloths off her nephew. Those songs, IMO, are extremely cheesy and very 90's. If the girls are very persistent about it and the groom is cool with it, then I compromise by playing Hot In Herre – Nelly. But that's as far as it goes. If you are a funny guy, then you can get away with having a sign hanging off the side of your booth (where the people walk up to request songs) that says something like "I will not play The Bird dance". When people request it, just ask them to read the posted sign. Sometimes you'll get a chuckle and they'll change their request.

The very odd time, you may encounter a situation where a person will request a song that they don't know the exact name of, so they will guess and get it wrong. Or they are genuinely mistaken as to the actual name. Or perhaps they've requested a song that you are not familiar with, even though you already have it in your music library. The best thing that you can do is to get them to listen to the song so they can confirm that it is the correct one they've requested. Load the song up on your pre-cueing track and let them wear the headphones. This is another example of excellent customer service that all mobile DJs should consider because it reflects on the company you work for and builds great customer relations that carry over to future events. But most importantly, it could make or break a great music set. The last thing you want is to accidently play a different song with the same name, only to have that same person come back to the booth to let you know that you've just played the wrong song. Total DJ fail. A perfect example of this was when Lana Del Ray came out with the song Summer Time Sadness. A girl requested this song to the rookie DJ that never attended the club scene and was unfamiliar with how popular it was. He cued up the song and played it without even listening to it first! Big mistake. He played the original track by Del Ray which is very slow and somber, essentially draining all the energy from the dance floor. The girl had actually wanted to hear the Cedric Gervais Remix that was very popular in the dance clubs at the time, but this rookie DJ didn't know that! The absolute worst thing he could've done is blame it on her when she came storming back to the DJ booth, but instead, he showed great poise by apologizing and immediately finding the correct song. So make sure you understand exactly which version of the song the requester is asking for. YouTube is infamous for having music videos posted with the wrong title or artist name attached to it, which causes much confusion if this is the only source that a person has listened to the song.

Pro Secret: Being a mobile DJ is a business where the customer is always right. Treat it as such. People paid good money to have you there, not the other way around. If people paid money to just come see you, then it's open game on creativity and boundary pushing because if they don't like you, they'll just leave. But at weddings, you are a special invited guest to please their friends and families.

Line Dances & Special Dances

THESE ARE DANCES that have their own dance moves that go along with the song. Depending on your area, some line dances will be more popular than others. Dances such as The Hustle, Slap Leather, Cotton-Eyed Joe, Cha-Cha Slide, or Macarena are taught at dance schools and even elementary or high schools, so there is a high probability that someone will know how to dance it. You only need a few good dancers to get it started and lots will follow. I encourage you to learn the most popular ones in your area so that you can get out on the floor and teach some people how to do it. The kids love it and the parents really appreciate the involvement. If you can dance it well, you'll earn a few extra great testimonials. It really pays to keep your eyes open for the newest dances.

Special dances are songs that have their own dance, but are not necessarily a line dance. This would include songs like Gangnam Style –Psy, Watch Me (whip/Nae Nae) – Silento, or Crank That – Soulja Boy. The young children really like these, so try to play them earlier in the night. Some people will actually rehearse these moves, just to perform them at the wedding, so if they request it, make sure you play it. The only problem with these is that they can get overplayed and most people will start to loath even hearing them. But if you have a super cute five year old that nails all the moves, then it'll turn into a winner. It even pays to know all these dance moves because often times, most people can't remember them and will look towards the DJ to see if he is involved and having fun too. Knowing the difference between a Duff and a Bop can actually get hired for another gig.

These dances are very popular because they have easy to learn choreographed dances moves. The main reason why most people do not dance is that they don't know how to dance. But as soon as you play a song that only has 5 dance moves that you repeat over and over, it takes away their reason of not knowing how to do the dance. A song such as the Cha Cha Slide will even say the dance moves throughout the song. It's kind of like a modern day square dance in the way the singer is directing the dancers what to do.

> **Pro Secret:** People will dance if they know how to do the dance moves.

All of these dances and songs are available to watch for free on YouTube, so you really don't have any excuse not to learn them in between performances.

I try and save these songs for an emergency or keep them in my back pocket if the dance floor starts to dwindle. A super great secret that I use is to utilize hash tags. If the wedding couple has a special hash tag for twitter, then you can send out a tweet letting people know when to rush the dance floor for a flash line dance. Tweet something like "Cha-Cha slide in 10 minutes. Spread the word to fill the floor #TimandTorriWedding" If done properly, you can have a hundred people rush the floor all at the same time. Super cool dance that the bride and groom will be talking about for many years!

> **Pro Secret:** Team up with your local dance studio and shoot a video on how to do the dance moves to different line dances. Posting this video on your website will bolster the fact that you are an expert wedding DJ. The local studio will also love it because it promotes both of your businesses.

Memorable Moments

BE ON THE LOOKOUT for memorable moments that happen during the wedding. This is a party, and all great parties have unique moments happen that people will talk about for years to come. As a DJ, you can enhance the drama of these moments or downplay and deescalate situations that may arise.

Let us look at few real life examples to learn from, that I've dealt with at weddings. A professional wedding DJ knows that if you are paying attention, then you will learn something new from every gig you perform at. The first DJ gig I ever played taught me many lessons including one in particular that I will never forget. The wedding was booked for a Wednesday night in small hotel basement. I did not charge much money because it was my very first gig ever. I even had to travel three hours to get there and they were not paying for accommodations either, so I had to drive right back home after the gig. I booked this gig for the reason being that if I messed up horribly, then maybe word would spread that quickly back to my main performing area. When I arrived at the venue, the bride and groom welcomed me and made it very clear that it was a going to be a laid back wedding. There was to be no speeches, garter belts or bouquet tosses. Then they proceeded to tell me that I should play "hard core, badass rap" all night long. Now I try to never judge anybody by appearances, but the groom was wearing sneakers and a tuxedo print T-shirt, all the bridesmaids had lower back tattoos, and most of the wedding party was beyond their limit of alcohol tolerance. When the dance portion started, I did like they requested and played everything from Jeezy and 2 Chainz, to Tupac and Young Money. I had no problem with this because I'm a big fan these artists and the dance floor was packed with a high energy group. Within two hours into the dance, a full fist flying fight broke out, the police showed up, arrested a wedding guest that had outstanding warrants and the hotel manager came to shut down the entire wedding early. I was back home by 2am and luckily still got paid.

I failed miserably on so many fronts, but I learned more from that first wedding than I did from all the research and books I read about DJing weddings. First of all, I kicked the party into high gear right at the start. This may be great to do in clubs or graduation parties, but it left me nowhere to go except down once people get tired on the floor. The second biggest mistake was not noticing what was gradually boiling up on the dance floor. If I would've noticed the stern looks, shoving, and people pushing others apart, then I could've toned down the aggressive music to help defuse a situation that ended horribly.

> **Pro Secret:** Look up and out to the dance floor often. Don't stay buried in your deck or you'll miss what's really happening at the party.

Another example was from a wedding that had a great big dance circle happening. Forty people were clapping in time with the music and taking turns doing their goofiest or coolest dance moves in the center of the circle. Beware of 90's Hip-Hop; it seems to always bring out The Running Man, The Shopping Cart, and The Sprinkler. It was half way through a Run DMC song that two people from exact opposite sides were entering the circle to do their dance moves, expect they were both walking backwards and didn't know the other person was walking toward the center at the same time. The moment right before they would've bumped into each other, one of the two guys broke into The Cabbage Patch dance and the other guy did a super high backwards flip. They crashed into each other and back flip guy did a nasty face plant. This qualifies as a memorable moment. Not all memorable moments will be positive or funny, but people will definitely be talking about them the next day. I witnessed this happen and was able to stop the music for brief moment, not to highlight the fact that this guy had a terrible accident, but to make sure that he was going to get proper medical attention. If he suffered a fractured vertebra in the neck, then it would be very important to immobilize him and call for an ambulance. Surprisingly, this can be neglected if the party keeps on rocking.

Conclusion

THAT was a lot of ground we covered on a small but very important topic. I encourage you to reread it and commit some of the details to memory so that when it comes time to perform, it will pop into your mind. I'm going to stress it again that most of your work needs to be done before the performance. If everything is organized and you know where/how to find any song in a hurry, then you're a step closer to becoming the best wedding DJ possible. It is easy to get wrapped up in a party and keep playing the same old songs, and when you want to try something new, it can be difficult to recall the names of some obscure tracks that don't get played much. Therefore, I encourage you to frequently update your list. Find new favorites and work them in slowly. You don't have to try an entire set of untested songs. Sprinkle them throughout the night and make a note of which ones worked and why. I have two separate playlists of songs that are new to me. One contains current songs from the past three months and the other contains old songs that I just haven't been fully introduced to. I listen to these playlists often on my own time.

Try to think of the reception as a play or a movie and you're the director. It's your job to make the party come to life. Slowly build up the energy levels and gradually create excitement to elevate the party to a higher level at each stage of the night. At the end of the night, people should be wanting more and not want the party to stop. If this is the case, then give yourself a pat on the back for a job well done.

Try to meet people's expectations, but also try to go out there and create new trends in the wedding DJ biz. Young adults that go to five weddings in a summer, start to dread attending them because they know exactly what to expect from a wedding DJ that is uncreative. Slowly work in new trends/games/dances and slowly phase out the old ones. We seriously don't need the Macarena around anymore, even though older folks will expect to hear it. Switch it out for a new popular dance. And if you do it enough times, people will start to ask for the new one. Let's put some new fun into weddings.

Lastly, thank you for purchasing and taking the time to read this brief book. I hope it will benefit you for years to come. If you use these methods properly, then you will stand out from your competition and get plenty of work at a higher price, and the wedding guests will love you for making weddings fun again!

If you would like to contact me, please visit my website www.djrichyroy.com. I'd love to hear from you and I look forward to helping out all my fellow wedding DJs.

Appendix

AUTHOR'S NOTE: The internet is filled with wedding song lists that stay up to date. I've included these few lists as reference to the content in the book. Also, these lists will most likely me different depending on your area of work. This represents the Sask, Canada area.

Top 100 Songs

1. 1999 – Prince
2. Amazed – Lonestar
3. At Last – Etta James
4. Baby Got Back – Sir Mix a Lot
5. Billie Jean – Michael Jackson
6. Bird Dance – Walter Ostanek
7. Boot Scootin Boogie – Brooks & Dunn
8. Brick House – Commodores
9. Brown Eyed Girl – Van Morrison
10. Build Me Up Buttercup – Foundations
11. Bust A Move – Young M.C.
12. Cadillac Ranch – Nitty Gritty Dirt Band
13. Can't Help Falling in Love – Elvis Presley
14. Celebration – Kool & the Gang
15. Cha Cha Slide – Casper
16. Chattahoochie – Alan Jackson
17. Cherry Bomb – John Cougar Mellancamp
18. Cotton Eyed Joe – Rednex

19. Cupid Shuffle – Cupid
20. Dancing In The Dark – Bruce Springsteen
21. Dancing Queen – ABBA
22. Don't Stop Believing – Journey
23. Dust on the Bottle – David Lee Murphy
24. Electric Slide – Marcia Griffiths
25. Fight for Your Right – Beastie Boys
26. Fishing in The Dark – Nitty Gritty Dirt Band
27. Footloose – Kenny Loggins
28. Friends In Low Places – Garth Brooks
29. Gangnam Style – PSY
30. Get Down Tonight – KC & Sunshine Band
31. Get Low – Lil' John and East Side Boyz
32. Get Up – James Brown
33. Girls Just Want to Have Fun – Cyndi Lauper
34. Give Me Everything Tonight – Pitbull
35. Gold Digger – Kanye West
36. Gonna Make You Sweat – C&C Music Factory
37. Grease Megamix – J. Travolta & O. John
38. Guitar Town – Steve Earl
39. Hey Baby – DJ Ozee
40. Hooked On a Feeling – Blue Swede
41. I Gotta Feeling – Black Eyed Peas
42. I Wanna Dance With Somebody – W.Houston
43. Ice Ice Baby – Vanilla Ice
44. Ignition (Remix) – R. Kelly
45. In The Mood – Glenn Miller

46. Its Tricky – Run DMC
47. Jessie's Girl – Rick Springfield
48. Jump Around – House of Pain
49. Jump On It – Sugarhill Gang
50. Jump, Jive, and Wail – Brian Setzer
51. Keep Your Hands To Yourself – Georgia Satellites
52. Let's Get it On – Marvin Gaye
53. Livin' on a Prayer – Bon Jovi
54. Love Shack – B-52's
55. Low – Flo Rida
56. Macarena '96 – Wil Veloz
57. Margaritaville – Jimmy Buffett
58. Mony Mony – Billy Idol
59. Moves Like Jagger – Maroon 5
60. Mustang Sally – Joe Cocher
61. No Diggity – Blackstreet
62. Old Time Rock and Roll – Bob Seger
63. One Dance – Drake
64. Party Rock Anthem – LMFAO
65. Play That Funky Music – Wild Cherry
66. Pour Some Sugar On Me – Def Leppard
67. Respect – Aretha Franklin
68. Rock and Roll All Night – KISS
69. Save a Horse, Ride a Cowboy – Big & Rich
70. Sexy and I Know It – LMFAO
71. Sexyback – Justin Timberlake

72. Shake It Off – Taylor Swift
73. Shout – Isley Brothers
74. Single Ladies – Beyonce
75. Somebody Like You – Keith Urban
76. Stayin' Alive – BeeGees
77. Sugar Pie Honey Bunch – Four Tops
78. Sweet Caroline – Neil Diamond
79. Sweet Child O' Mine – Guns N' Roses
80. Sweet Home Alabama – Lynard Skynard
81. The Twist – Chubby Checker
82. The Way You Look Tonight – Frank Sinatra
83. Thriller – Michael Jackson
84. Tootsie Roll – 69 Boyz
85. Treasure – Bruno Mars
86. Twist and Shout – Beatles
87. Unchained Melody – Righteous Brothers
88. Unforgettable – Nat King Cole
89. Uptown Funk – Bruno Mars
90. Wagon Wheel – Darius Rucker
91. Wake Me Up Before You Go Go – Wham!
92. We're Here for a Good Time – Trooper
93. What a Wonderful World – Louis Armstrong
94. What I Like About You – Romantics
95. When The Sun Goes Down – Kenny Chesney
96. White Houses – Vanessa Carlton
97. Wonderful Tonight – Eric Clapton
98. Yeah! – Usher

99. YMCA – Village People

100. You Shook Me All Night Long – AC/DC

Line Dances & Special Dance Songs

1. Achy Breaky Heart – Billy Ray Sirus
2. Any Man of Mine – Shania Twain
3. Boot Scootin' Boogie – Brooks and Dunn
4. Bunny Hop – Ray Anthony
5. Butterfly Dance - Emeralds
6. Cadillac Ranch – Nitty Gritty Dirt Band
7. Chicken Dance (Bird Dance) Emeralds
8. Conga – Gloria Estefan
9. Copperhead Road – Steve Earl
10. Cotton Eyed Joe - Rednex
11. Crank That – Soulja Boy Tell 'Em
12. Cupid's Shuffle - Cupid
13. Da Dip
14. Electric Slide – Marcia Griffiths
15. Gangnam Style - Psy
16. Heel N' Toe Polka – The Ukrainian Oldtimers
17. Hoedown Throwdown
18. Jump In The Line – Harry Belafonte
19. Locomotion – Kylie Minogue or Little Eva
20. Macarena – Wil Veloz or Los Del Rio
21. Party Rock Anthem - LMFAO
22. Redneck Girl – Bellamy Brothers
23. Rock Lobster – The B-52's
24. Shout – The Isley Brothers
25. Teach Me How To Dougie – Cali Swag Distric

26. The Cha Cha Slide – MC Jig
27. The Harlem Shake - Baauer
28. The Hustle – Van McCoy
29. The Limbo Rock – Chubby Checker
30. The Stroll
31. The Twist – Chubby Checker
32. The Wobble – V.I.C.
33. Thriller – Michael Jackson
34. Time Warp – Rocky Horror Picture Show
35. Tush Push
36. Wagon Wheel – Darius Rucker
37. Watch Me (Whip/Nae Nae)
38. Watermelon Crawl – Tracy Bird
39. What the Cowgirls Do – Vince Gill
40. Y.M.C.A. – Village People

Last Songs

1. (I've Had) The Time of My Life
    – Bill Medley & Jennifer Warnes
2. All Night Long – Lionel Richie
3. All You Need is Love - Beatles
4. Always – Bon Jovi
5. At Last – Etta James
6. Best Day of My Life – American Authors
7. Bohemian Rhapsody – Queen
8. Closing Time – Semisonic
9. Don't Stop Believing - Journey
10. Evacuate the Dancefloor - Cascada
11. Everybody Needs Somebody To Love
    – The Blues Brothers
12. Friends in Low Places – Garth Brooks
13. Good Riddance (Time of Your Life)
    – Green Day
14. Hit The Road Jack – Ray Charles
15. Ho Hey - Lumineers
16. I Cross My Heart – George Strait
17. I Don't Want This Night to End
    – Luke Bryan
18. I Don't Want to Miss a Thing - Aerosmith
19. Ignition (Remix) – R. Kelly
20. It's the End of the World – R.E.M.
21. Just The Two of Us – Bill Withers

22. Just the Way You Are – Bruno Mars
23. Last Dance – Donna Summer
24. My Best Friend – Tim McGraw
25. Na Na Hey Hey Kiss Him Goodbye
    - Steam
26. Never Forget – Take That
27. Not Ready to Go – The Trews
28. One More Time – Daft Punk
29. Piano Man – Billy Joel
30. Save the Best for Last – Vanessa Williams
31. Save the Last Dance For Me   –M. Buble
32. Shout – Isley Brothers
33. Shut Up and Dance – Walk the Moon
34. Sweet Caroline – Neil Diamond
35. Take Me Home Tonight – Eddie Money
36. Take My Drunk Ass Home – Luke Bryan
37. The Last Dance – Frank Sinatra
38. The Party's Over – Willie Nelson
39. Thinking Out Loud – Ed Sheeran
40. Today Was A Fairytale – Taylor Swift
41. Unforgettable – Natalie Cole
42. Wasn't That A Party – Irish Rovers
43. We Are Family – Sister Sledge
44. We Are Young – FUN.
45. We Can't Stop – Miley Cyrus
46. Wonderful Tonight – Eric Clapton

47. You Are The Best Thing
    – Ray Lamontagne
48. You Shook Me All Night Long – AC/DC
49. You're My Best Friend – Queen
50. Young, Wild, and Free
    – Snoop Dogg & Wiz Khalifa

Grand Entrances

1. AC/DC – Thunderstruck
2. Adventure of a Lifetime – Coldplay
3. Another One Bites The Dust – Queen
4. Avicii – Levels
5. Beautiful Day – U2
6. Bittersweet Symphony – The Verve
7. Bring 'Em Out – T.I. Feat. Jay Z
8. Can't Stop The Feeling – Justin Timberlake
9. Celebration – Kool & The Gang
10. Get The Party Started – P!nk
11. Gonna Fly Now (Rocky Theme) – B Conti
12. Good To Be Alive (Hallelujah) – A. Grammar
13. I Believe In a Thing Called Love – Darkness
14. I Gotta Feeling – Black Eyed Peas
15. I'm Shipping Up To Boston
    – Dropkick Murphys
16. Let's Get It Started – Black Eyed Peas
17. Rather Be – Clean Bandit
18. Signed, Sealed, Delivered, I'm Yours
    – Stevie Wonder
19. Sugar – Maroon 5
20. The Way You Make Me Feel – M. Jackson
21. This Is How We Roll – Florida Georgia Line
22. Uptown Funk – Bruno Mars
23. Walk This Way – Run DMC and Aerosmith

24. Welcome To The Jungle – Guns N' Roses
25. You Make My Dreams Come True
    – Hall & Oates

ABOUT THE AUTHOR

DJ Richy Roy lives in Weyburn, Saskatchewan, Canada. He has a wonderful wife, three beautiful children, and a very laid back fish named Thurston. When he's not spinning tunes, he's enjoying life by cooking, writing, parenting, reviewing movies, and performing magic.

Printed in Great Britain
by Amazon